In this glossary:

[a] is pronounced as in f<u>a</u>r
[e] is pronounced as in g<u>e</u>t
[ee] is pronounced as in f<u>ee</u>t
[i] is pronounced as in s<u>i</u>t
[o] is pronounced as between g<u>o</u>t and g<u>oa</u>t
[oo] is pronounced as in l<u>oo</u>se
[y] is pronounced as in <u>y</u>es

[kh] is pronounced as in Scottish lo<u>ch</u>
[zh] is pronounced as in vi<u>si</u>on

Other books available from Ethnic Enterprises:

The Raspberry Hut
and Other Ukrainian Folk Tales Retold in English
by Danny Evanishen

Vuiko Yurko The First Generation
by Danny Evanishen

I Can't Find the Words to Tell You
by Anne Everatt

Zhabka

and Other Ukrainian Folk Tales Retold in English

Edited by Danny Evanishen
Translations by John W Evanishen
Illustrations by Deanna Evanishen

Published by
Ethnic Enterprises
Publishing Division
Summerland, BC

Copyright © 1995
Daniel W Evanishen

All rights reserved. The use of any part of this publication reproduced, transmitted in any form by any means, electronic, mechanical, photocopying, recording, or otherwise, or stored in any retrieval system, without the prior written consent of the publisher is an infringement of the copyright law.

Canadian Cataloguing in Publication Data

Main entry under title:
   Zhabka, and other Ukrainian folk takes retold in English

ISBN 0-9697748-3-4

1. Tales--Ukraine. I. Evanishen, Danny, 1945-
GR203.18.Z52 1995   398.2'0947'71   C95-910181-0

Ethnic Enterprises
Publishing Division
Box 1324
Summerland, BC
V0H 1Z0

Printed and Bound in Canada
by New Horizon Printers
Summerland, BC

1 2 3 4 5 6 7 8 9 10 • 04 03 02 01 2000 1999 98 97 96 95

Table of Contents

The Adopted Father	11
Adventure in the Woods	21
The Bear and the Fiddler	25
The Big Round Bun	29
Danylo Burmylo, the Bear	35
The Dog and the Wolf	40
The Goat and the Ram	47
The Greedy Daughters	53
The Hedgehog and the Hare	56
The Holy Icon	61
Ivan Pobyvan	65
Kyrylo the Tanner	75
The Magic Chest	83
Okh	94
A Visit in the Grave	113
Zhabka	125
Notes on the Tales	128

For my mother, Natalka Evanishen, who told me my first folk tales.

Foreword

This book is the second volume in this series. Eventually, all the folk tales in my collection will be printed. That should take many more volumes and many years to do. After four years of collecting, I have almost two hundred tales. There could be as many as four thousand yet to find.

Collecting and publishing these tales is a labor of love. I find that it is more than just work (although that is considerable); it is also enjoyment. I am having fun.

As in the first volume, *The Raspberry Hut*, some of the tales to be found in this book are old favorites, while others are less familiar.

If anyone has any more tales they would like to contribute to future volumes, they could be sent to me at this address:

> Danny Evanishen
> Box 1324
> Summerland, BC
> V0H 1Z0.

—Danny Evanishen, Editor

Acknowledgments

This book, like the first in the series, is the result of a lot of work by a number of people.

John W Evanishen, my father, did the translations and gave me much guidance. Natalka Evanishen, my mother, provided my introduction to folk tales when I was a child and is always there with encouragement. Deanna Evanishen, my niece, did all of the art work.

Thanks are due to the many libraries and archives that made their material available to me. A list of all the stories and their sources will be published once the collection is complete.

Special thanks are due to Professor JB Rudnyckyj for material from his book *Ukrainian-Canadian Folklore in English Translation*, and to Dr Robert Klymasz for permission to use material from his book *Folk Narrative Among Ukrainian-Canadians in Western Canada*. I appreciate the efforts of those who have gone before and are willing to share their work with the rest of us.

A number of people have written to me with their stories. When the stories submitted by these people are published, I will at that time acknowledge their contributions.

Thank you also to Dorene Fehr, who did much reading and advising on the project, and also took the photograph on the back cover.

— Danny Evanishen, Editor

The Adopted Father

Once there were three brothers who were orphans. They had neither mother nor father, nor any family at all, except each other. They had no land, no house, nothing. Being so unlucky, they decided to go out into the world and work for others. On their way, not long after they had started out, they met an old man with a long white beard.

"Whither are you bound, my children?" the old man asked.

"Unfortunately, Dido, we are not your children, nor are we the children of anyone else living. The truth is, we are orphans, and we are looking for someone to work for," they replied.

"Have you no land and no house or anything of your own?" the old man asked.

"No," said the three brothers. "We are alone in the world and own nothing. We would like to find someone to work for that we could think of as our own father."

"Well, good," said the old man. "If you come and work for me, I will be a father to you. If you do as I teach, you will learn how to live a good life. I will teach you to be truthful and to follow the right path to a good and a happy life."

The three brothers agreed to this and followed the old man. They travelled through dense forests and across vast open plains and, as they walked, they saw in the distance a pretty house which was small and painted white. As they came closer, they could see that it was in a cherry orchard and was surrounded by beautiful flower gardens.

Nearing the house, they saw a pretty girl standing in the doorway. The oldest son saw the girl and said: "This is the kind of girl who would make my happiness for life if I could marry her. If I had such a wife and some cows and oxen I could have a good life."

"Then let us go and woo her for you," said the old man. "I will act as your matchmaker. You will marry the girl, and the cows and oxen will come in time. You will indeed be happy, but you must not forget to lead a righteous life."

The girl heard them out and accepted the proposal, and the two were soon married. The oldest son became the master of the land and the couple started their happy life together.

The old man and the two remaining brothers continued their journey. They came upon a flour mill by a stream and saw a beautiful young girl in the garden. The second son saw her and said: "This is the kind of girl who would make my happiness for life if I could marry her. I could work in this mill and be happy for the rest of my life."

The old man said, "If that is what you wish, it will be so. I will be your matchmaker."

The girl heard and accepted the offer, and she and the second son were married. They lived by the mill and the husband worked for the miller, who was the father of the girl.

"Now, my son, you can live happily," said the old man. "But you must never forget to do what is fair and right."

The old man and the youngest son bade them farewell and went on their way. They came upon a poor but neat old house and, there, they stopped to rest. A girl came out of the house and greeted them graciously. She was dressed very poorly; her clothing had patches upon patches. However, she was very cheerful and bright.

The remaining son said: "I would like to marry this happy girl. We could work together and make ourselves a good life. With a wife like this I know that I would be very happy. We two could care for ourselves and also for those who are in more need than we are."

The girl and the youngest son were soon married, and the old man departed, saying to them,

"Live well and live happily, but do not forget always to do what is just and right."

The three brothers lived their separate lives and they prospered. The eldest brother operated a successful farm. He built large brick buildings and began to amass much wealth. He soon began to think of nothing but the success of the farm, and he started to hoard the wealth he was accumulating. He became very stingy and miserly in his habits.

The second brother also became wealthy. Because the miller had died, he had taken over the mill. The hired hands did all the work while he lay around eating, drinking, sleeping, giving orders and dreaming of his wealth.

Meanwhile, the youngest brother and his wife lived together very simply and very happily. They had little, but what little they had was shared with others who had less, and they always had words of good cheer for everybody.

The adopted father of the three brothers made plans to visit his sons. "Let us see how they are getting along," he said, "and whether they live righteously."

The old man trimmed his beard so he would not be recognized, dressed in his shabbiest clothes and went to visit. He found his oldest son walking in his yard admiring his farm.

The old man bowed before the brother and said, "I beg your pardon, Master, but could you help a poor old man in need of assistance?"

"You are not so old," was the reply. "If you need help, go and earn it. I got myself up on my feet not long ago, and I cannot spare any help."

The old man could see all the wealth in the yard: the large brick buildings, the bulging granaries, the full stables and the fields crowded with cattle. He turned and walked away and, when he was a short distance down the road, he turned to look at the farm and all its riches.

As the old man stared and stared, the whole farm suddenly went up in flames and was completely destroyed.

Arriving at the home of the second son, the old man saw the bustling mill, the huge millpond and the prosperous household.

As he entered the mill, the old man bowed before the second brother and said, "I beg your pardon, Master, but could you help a poor old man in need of assistance?"

"Well, now," said the middle brother. "I myself work very hard for what you see here, and I am not wealthy enough to spare anything for the likes of you."

The old man walked down the road. He turned to look at the mill and, as he stared and stared, the mill and the house went up in flames.

Finally arriving at the home of the youngest son, the old man saw that the house, although it was small and poor, was neat and tidy. The brother was dressed in clothing that was poor but clean, and he smiled as he greeted the old man.

"I beg your pardon, Master, but could you help a poor old man in need of assistance?" said the old man.

"Please come into our house," said the youngest son. "We will feed you as well as we are able and give you some food to take with you on your journey."

When the girl saw how shabbily the old man was dressed, she felt sorry for him. She brought him a clean pair of pants and a shirt that she had just mended.

After they had eaten their meal, the three sat on the bench in the front of the house.

"Tell me what your plans are," said the son. "You are welcome to stay with us for some time and consider your future."

"Thank you, no," said the old man. "Unfortunately, I have received a mortal wound and I have but one day to live."

"Oh no!" cried the girl. "Is there no remedy for this wound?"

"There is one," replied the old man, "but no one will give me what is required, although everyone is capable of giving it."

The youngest son asked the old man, "Why would people not give, if they could? And what is it that is needed?"

"It is necessary that the owner of a home burn his own home to the ground and then rub the ashes in my wound. That is the only way I can ever be healed."

"Well, my dear wife, what do you think?" asked the son.

"Oh yes," she replied. "We can always build another home but, when a good man dies, he will never live again."

"Very well," said the son. "Let us get the children out of the house and begin."

The youngest son looked at his home and felt sad to see it burn, but he felt more sorry for the old man. He set fire to the house, and the flames soon engulfed it.

As they watched it burn, they could see a large new house rising out of the smoke and ashes. What kind of miracle was this?

The old man sat on a stump and smiled to himself as the youngest brother and his family buzzed around with excitement.

"Of my three adopted sons, only you, the youngest, kept to the path of righteousness," said the old man. "May you live in happiness all the rest of your days."

The youngest son then recognized his adopted father and came to embrace him, but he put his arms around only thin air. The old man had vanished.

Adventure in the Woods

The father of a family left his farm and went in search of work, leaving behind his wife with their son and daughter, who were ten years old and six. One evening soon after, the mother told the children to go and fetch the cattle from the forest. They were good children, and they immediately set out to find the cows.

They wandered through the woods, but could hear no cow-bells. Finally, it got dark and they realized they were lost. They were not worried, so they stopped under a tree, lit a fire to keep warm, and began to doze off.

Suddenly, they heard a crackling sound in the forest. The children were frightened and huddled together. As they sat shaking, a bear came to the edge of the firelight and stood there looking at the children and the fire. He stood for a while and then disappeared into the bushes.

The children were afraid to move. The fire was almost out, but they were too scared to go and look for more wood, so they sat there and held onto each other.

After a short time, they heard another crackling noise in the forest. Again, the bear appeared but, this time, he was walking on his hind legs and he had in his arms a load of dry firewood. He walked to the edge of the almost-out campfire and dumped his armload directly onto it. He waited until the fire was blazing merrily and then turned and disappeared into the forest forever.

The Bear and the Fiddler

Once a poor peasant was being punished for something. Whether he was guilty or not does not matter here, but the punishment does. His sentence was that he was to be thrown into a cave with a wild bear. For his last request, he was allowed to take his fiddle with him.

Upon entering the cave, the man began to play his fiddle, sweetly, sadly and mournfully. He was sure that his time on this earth was over and he tried to make his last few moments as pleasant as possible.

The bear came to the man and sat down to listen to the music. He had never heard such a beautiful thing before.

"If you teach me to play like that," said the bear, "I will set you free."

The man was surprised to hear this but, being quick-witted enough, he said to the bear: "It would be very difficult for you to play, because your paws are not the right shape to hold the fiddle properly."

"If that is so, then I am afraid that I will have to eat you," said the bear as he stood up.

"But we could straighten your paws," the man said hurriedly. "We would have to put your fingers under a heavy weight to straighten them, but the pain would be worth it, for then you could hold the fiddle and learn to play."

"Let it be so," said the bear.

The man rolled a huge boulder onto the paws of the bear and then stood back. The bear was whimpering with the pain, but he gritted his teeth and did not cry out.

When he was sure the bear was safely trapped, the man picked up his fiddle and prepared to leave. As he left the cave, the man turned back and said to the bear: "Wiser folk than I am have said that one should not try to be what one is not. A bear can be no more than a bear; he cannot be a fiddler because he has not the brains of a man. And so, farewell, my friend."

The Big Round Bun

Once there lived an old man and an old woman. They had eaten all their bread, and the old man began to beg his wife, "Baba, will you please bake us a nice big round loaf of bread?"

Baba said, "From what can I bake it, Dido, when there is no flour?"

"Sweep the bottom of the flour bin and maybe you can find enough to make one loaf."

Baba swept the bottom of the bin, gathered up all the flour she could find and Dido fired up the pich. She made as much dough as she could, which was only enough for one Big Round Bun. Dido baked the Big Round Bun and Baba put it on the windowsill to cool.

The Big Round Bun sat cooling for a while, then rolled down onto the bench outside the house. From the bench, he bounced onto the ground; then he rolled through the gate and away he went down the road.

As he rolled down the road, he met a Rabbit who said, "Big Round Bun, Big Round Bun, I am going to eat you up."

"Do not eat me, Little Rabbit; I will sing you a song."

"Oh ho! You are a singing Bun, are you? Very well; let us hear your song."

The Big Round Bun sang:

"I was swept from a bin,
I was baked in a tin.
I ran from my maker,
And I ran from my baker,
And now, from the likes of you
I will run away, too!"

The Big Round Bun rolled away and the Rabbit could not catch him. Down the road, he met a Wolf who said, "Big Round Bun, Big Round Bun, I am going to eat you up."

"Do not eat me, Brother Wolf; I will sing you a song."

"Very well; sing for me."

The Big Round Bun sang:

"I was swept from a bin,
I was baked in a tin.
I ran from my maker,
And I ran from my baker,
And now, from the likes of you
I will run away, too! "

The Big Round Bun rolled away and the Wolf could not catch him. Down the road, he met a Bear who said, "Big Round Bun, Big Round Bun, I am going to eat you up."

"Oh no, do not eat me, Big Bear; I will sing you a song."

"Well, okay; let us hear your song."

The Big Round Bun sang:

"I was swept from a bin,
I was baked in a tin.
I ran from my maker,
And I ran from my baker,
And now, from the likes of you
I will run away, too!"

The Big Round Bun rolled away and the Bear could not catch him. Down the road, he met a Fox who said, "Big Round Bun, Big Round Bun, I am going to eat you up."

"Do not eat me, Little Sister Fox; I will sing you a song."

"Okay, but I am hard of hearing," said the Fox. "Sit on my nose so I can hear you better."

The Big Round Bun hopped up onto the nose of the Fox and was just starting to sing when the Fox went "Chomp!" and ate him up.

Danylo Burmylo, the Bear

One day, a man was in the woods loading his cart with firewood, when he saw a large bear coming towards him.

"Good day to you, Danylo Burmylo," said the man. "And how are you today?"

"Good day to you," said Danylo Burmylo. "I must find myself a place to hide."

"Hide?" said the man. "Who from?"

"Not from any creature in the forest, as you well know," said the bear. "I must hide myself from the coming winter."

"What have you to fear?" asked the man. "You are so big and strong. Are you not stronger than winter?"

"What I can seize with my paws and crush, I do not fear. If I could do so with winter, I would finish it and never have to go hungry again," said the bear.

"Imagine that — a bear going hungry," said the man. "Not that a little religious fasting would not do your soul some good. You have sinned enough, God knows, by eating many sheep."

"Do people not kill sheep for food?" asked the bear. "Is it a sin only when a bear does it? Mostly, I eat berries and roots and the little vermin which damage your garden. Of course, when there is nothing else about, I must live, so I eat a sheep.

"I am far worse off than you people are in winter, too. You have stored your firewood and your harvest long before winter arrives, and you have warm clothing to protect you from the howling wind and the cold. I have nothing to protect me except my thin skin, and that does not help very much.

"So you see, there is nothing I can do. I must find a warm den to hide in. That is what I am doing now," finished Danylo Burmylo.

"Yes, I see," said the man. "But how will you live, and what will you eat?"

"Bears do not need to eat in the winter," said Danylo Burmylo. "We store up a lot of fat over the summer and, while we sleep the winter away, we live on that. Of course, in the spring I will be just skin and bones, but I will survive. What I need the most is a warm place so that I do not freeze while I am asleep."

"You could come and live with me," said the man. "I will give you a warm place to live and enough to eat. In return I will ask that you tend my beehives in the summer."

Danylo Burmylo thought this over and agreed. He climbed into the cart and the two drove to the farm where the man lived. The man and Danylo Burmylo had a big bowl of borsch for supper and then went out to look at the barn.

The barn was as dark as any den the bear had seen, and it was warm enough for him. He thought himself lucky, indeed. Now he had a nice warm house, plenty of food, and nothing to do until summer. When summer came, he would be happy to tend the bees and have a little bit of honey every now and then.

The only problem was that the man put a large, thick chain on Danylo Burmylo to stop him from wandering about and frightening the rest of the animals on the farm. He would have to spend all of his time in the barn.

One day, as the man was bringing Danylo Burmylo his supper, a dog sneaked in and attacked Danylo Burmylo. The man had some trouble beating the dog away, but it made Danylo Burmylo think seriously about his life there. As well, there were cattle in the other end of the barn, and their angry snorting always startled him and woke him up.

Danylo Burmylo thought and thought and, finally, one evening, he asked the man to take off the chain so that he could go for a walk outside. It was cold and Danylo Burmylo shivered, but he stretched himself, took a few steps, and then turned to the man.

"I want to thank you for the food and the shelter and for your kindness," said Danylo Burmylo, "but I cannot stay here any longer."

With that, Danylo Burmylo ran straight off into the forest. When he had gone some distance, he sat down for a rest and said to himself: "Freedom, even with a little bit of hunger, is better than any well-fed captivity." For the rest of his life, he lived in the forest in freedom, just as bears are meant to do.

The Dog and the Wolf

Once there was a dog who was getting old and tired in the service of his master, who was a farmer. Seeing no further use for the dog, the master threw him out. The poor old dog roamed the fields feeling very sorry for himself. At length, he met up with a wolf.

"Why are you all alone out here and hungry?" asked the wolf.

"I have spent many faithful years guarding my master and his family," said the dog, "and now that I have grown old and weak, he has thrown me out to fend for myself."

"I think I can help you," said the wolf. "If you agree to my plan, your master will take you back into his heart and his house."

"I would like that very much," said the dog. "If it can be so, I will find a way to repay you."

"Here is my plan," said the wolf. "When your master and his wife go to the field to harvest their grain, they take their baby along. They put him to sleep beside a haystack while they are working. I will sneak up and run off with the baby; you will appear out of nowhere and chase me away and rescue the baby. They will be so pleased with you that they will take you back with tears in their eyes."

They both thought this would work and, when the master and his wife went to work in the field, they carried out their plan. The wolf grabbed the baby, and the dog, with great barking and yelping, chased after him and took the child away from him. The dog returned to the frantic parents with the baby, and the two of them were beside themselves with joy at this miraculous rescue.

The master hugged the dog and the mistress kissed him and they both fed the dog until he could eat no more.

"Thank you for saving our baby," they said. As the wolf had promised, they both had tears in their eyes.

For the rest of the day, the dog stood guard over the baby while the master and mistress worked in the field. When evening came, they all returned to the farmhouse together.

"Make an extra bowl of varennyky for our brave dog," said the master to his wife. "And put a big piece of bacon in the dish."

The master seated the dog beside him at the table. He personally served the dog, and even blew on the hot food so that the dog would not burn his mouth.

"This has all come about because of the wolf," thought the dog. "I must try to think of a way to repay him."

Some time after these events, the master was about to marry off his eldest daughter. He arranged a large party with much food and drink. The dog took note of these preparations and went into the fields to find the wolf.

"I have finally thought of a way to repay you," said the dog. "Tomorrow, my master is going to have a party with plenty of fancy food and drink. Come to the bushes in the garden and I will take you into the party, where you can eat and drink all you want."

Next day, the dog went to the bushes in the garden where he found the wolf. He sneaked the wolf into the house and hid him under the table. The dog then grabbed a large piece of meat and a bottle of wine from the kitchen, which he dragged under the table to the wolf.

The guests, thinking the dog meant to eat and drink all this himself, were surprised that the master allowed the dog to act thusly.

"This dog you see here today has done us a wonderful service," the master told his guests. "We will always be grateful to him."

The master told the story to the guests, who were very impressed. After that, the dog got many gentle pats on the head, many pieces of choice food, and many scratches behind his ears. The food, of course, he slipped to the wolf under the banquet table.

Later, the dog joined his friend under the table and found that the wolf had had too much wine to drink. He was starting to be affected by the joyous mood of the party.

"I feel so happy that I just have to sing," sighed the wolf.

"What? Sing? Are you crazy?" cried the dog. "No one must know you are here! Look, I have brought you some more wine. Drink it and stay quiet under here."

The wolf drank the wine but, of course, that only made him happier and more careless.

"I must sing! I must!" babbled the wolf.

"Shush yourself up," said the dog, "or we will pay for your foolishness with our lives."

"I cannot help myself," said the wolf. "I must sing, and I will."

The wolf threw back his head and let out a loud, eerie howl. At first, there was a shocked silence, and then a great furor erupted in the house. The frightened guests began running every which way and, in the commotion, the table was overturned. The guests, surprised as they were, grabbed pokers and knives and were about to kill the wolf when the quick-witted dog jumped on his back and pretended to be strangling him.

"Stand back!" cried the master. "If you try to kill the wolf you could hurt the dog. The dog has him in hand, anyway."

The dog tumbled the wolf out the door and chased him across the field. When they were out of sight of the house, they both stopped running and stood there, panting.

"You saved my life once," said the dog, "and now I believe I have repaid the favor."

The two said farewell and went their separate ways, never to meet again.

The Goat and the Ram

Once there lived a man and his wife, who owned a Goat and a Ram. The Ram was big and strong, but he was not very clever or brave, and the Goat, while he was not big and strong, was very clever and quite brave. The animals were great friends; everywhere the Goat went, the Ram went, too. When the Goat sneaked into the cabbage patch in the garden, the Ram would follow. And when the Goat jumped into the orchard, the Ram was right behind.

"We must be rid of these animals," said the man to his wife. "With them here, we can have no garden and no orchard." The wife agreed, and the man went out to talk to the animals.

"You two are more trouble than you are worth. You ruin our garden and our orchard and do nothing good for us. Leave this yard and do not come back."

When the Goat and the Ram heard these words, they hunted up a sack into which they put their few belongings, and hurriedly left.

They went across the field, not knowing where they were going. Suddenly, in the middle of the field, they saw the head of a dead Wolf.

"Pick up the head, Ram. You are the stronger one."

"No, Goat. You do it. You are the braver."

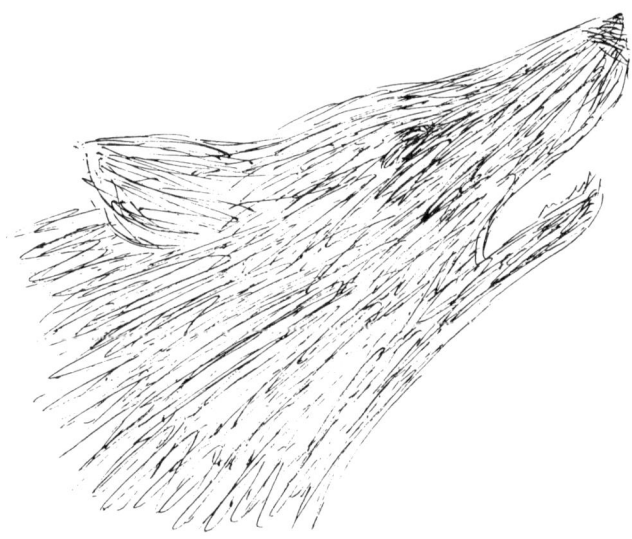

The two of them finally agreed to do it together, and they put the head of the Wolf into their sack. They walked on until they saw a fire burning in a hollow by some trees.

"Let us go there and spend the night by the fire, lest the Wolves come in the night and eat us up," said the Goat.

When they got to the fire they saw, to their dismay, three Wolves cooking porridge. The Wolves had also seen them, so they could do nothing but greet the Wolves. "Good health to you, young fellows," they said.

"We are all quite healthy, thank you," replied the Wolves gleefully. "Our porridge is just beginning to boil, and now we also have some meat for our supper."

This frightened the Goat, but the Ram had been frightened for a long time. The Goat scratched his head and began to think. At last, he whispered something to the Ram and then said loudly, "Ram, get out that Wolf head from our sack and we will cook it up for our supper."

The Ram got out the head and dragged it to the fire. "That is not the one I want," said the Goat. "Bring the big one."

The Ram went back into the sack, fished around a bit, and dragged the same head back to the fire. "No, no," said the Goat. "Let us have the biggest one."

The Wolves were quite amazed to see and hear all this. They became alarmed, and each tried to think how to get away from these two vicious Wolf-killers.

One Wolf said, "The porridge is boiling quite well, but it needs more water. I will go and get some." Off he went, thinking that he had very smartly saved his skin.

The second Wolf, after a short while, said, "That Wolf! He is so lazy! He went to get water, but I bet he is just sitting by the river, dreaming. The porridge needs the water, so I will go and hurry him up." Off went the second Wolf, happy to be alive.

The third Wolf became very worried. "I had better go see what is keeping those two," he said. "They may have run into trouble." Off he ran, also happy to have escaped the Wolf-killers.

The Goat said to the Ram, "Well, Brother Ram, we had better eat up the porridge and run away from here as fast as we can."

In the meantime, the Wolves were starting to come to their senses. They said, "There are three of us and only two of them. Imagine Wolves being afraid of Goats and Sheep! Let us go back there and eat them up."

By the time the Wolves got back, however, the Goat and the Ram were gone. They had run to the forest and were hiding up in an oak tree.

The Wolves trailed the Goat and the Ram, and finally found them in the oak tree. The Goat had climbed almost to the top and the Ram was sitting a bit lower.

The Wolves gathered around the tree and began to plan how they would get the Goat and the Ram down. One of the Wolves said to another: "You are the eldest and the most clever of us. Use some of your magic tricks to help us get those two out of the tree."

The eldest Wolf lay on his back with his legs sticking up in the air and began his magic. The Ram, who was trembling with fear, lost his grip and fell down right on top of the Wolf.

The Goat saw what had happened and quickly cried, "Grab that magician Wolf and hand him up to me!"

Hearing this, the startled Wolves jumped up and ran away as fast as they could, leaving a cloud of dust where they had been.

The Goat and the Ram now felt quite safe. They set up camp right there and are probably still there today.

The Greedy Daughters

An old man had provided for his two daughters as best he could. Although he was not wealthy, when they were married he divided all of his estate between the two of them. He was too old to work any more, so he thought they would provide for him while he lived.

As it was, however, neither daughter wanted the father to live with her, and the poor old man was shuffled from one house to another. This was very hard for the old man, so he went to the vorozhka to ask her advice.

"What can I do?" he asked. "I gave my land and all my worldly goods to my daughters, and now they treat me like a dog. I go from house to house and neither daughter wants me."

The vorozhka listened to the story and said: "Here is what you must do. Find a sack and put into it broken dishes and bits of metal and pieces of paper. Keep a tight grip on the sack all the time

and, when you are in bed, be sure to talk and mumble in your sleep."

The old man got a sack and put into it the things the vorozhka had told him to find. He held onto the sack all the time and mumbled in his sleep. The two daughters noticed the sack right away and held a conference. Suddenly, each wanted the old man to come and stay with her. The two finally agreed that when the old man died, they would divide the contents of the sack, and the old man could live wherever he wanted.

The old man lived peacefully with one of his daughters and often visited the other. Both daughters took very good care of the old man, and he spent the rest of his life in comfort, surrounded by his loving grandchildren. He always gripped the sack tightly and he always mumbled in his sleep.

When the old man finally died, the daughter called her sister to her house to arrange for the funeral and, of course, to open the sack. When they finally pried the sack out of the grasp of the old man and opened it, they were stunned. There was nothing in there but junk! They were angry that they had been fooled, but what could they do about it?

The Hedgehog and the Hare

Once there was a Hedgehog. Each morning, he came out of his home to look at the wide world. One day, he came out and said, "I think I will go to my field and see how my carrots and beets are growing."

Ambling along, he hummed a song to himself. Just then, a Hare jumped out from behind a bush; he was inspecting his own field to see how large his cabbages had grown.

"Oh," said the Hedgehog brightly. "Who is so speedy and is already on the field?"

"You!" retorted the bad-tempered Hare. "You are such a bandy-legs. Your father was a bandy-legs, your grandfather was a bandy-legs, so was your whole family, and so are you."

The Hedgehog was very surprised that for his cheery greeting he had received such a rude reply; he had been insulted right back as far as his father and grandfather!

The Hedgehog said to the Hare: "You are always making fun of people, and must be taught a lesson. Would you like to run a race with me? We will see who will win."

The Hare burst out laughing. "You? You want to race with me?"

"Yes," said the Hedgehog quietly. "I want to race with you."

"Well then," said the Hare, "let us go."

"No," said the Hedgehog, "not now. I must go home and tell my dear wife so she will know where I went."

The Hare was glad of this, as he was hungry. He said to himself: "This delay is good; I will have a feed of cabbage and will run much better. Not that it will be hard to outrun that poor old bandy-legs Hedgehog!"

When the Hedgehog got home he said to his wife, "Guess what is happening."

"What, my dear husband?"

"I have challenged the Hare to a race," he said. He told her everything.

"You are taking a big chance to race against that Hare," she said.

"Never fear, dear wife," said the Hedgehog, "it will turn out right. But I need your help. Get ready and come with me."

As they walked along, the Hedgehog told his wife what to do: "When we come to the field, you stay at this end, hidden in a furrow. When the Hare runs up, you say, 'I am already here!' We look so much alike that he will not know the difference. When he runs to the other end of the field I will shout, 'I am already here!'"

"Good," said his wife.

The Hedgehog walked over to the Hare at the far end of the field and said, "I am here, and I am ready to race."

"Then let us race."

The Hedgehog stood in one furrow and the Hare in the next one. One, two, three! and away they went. The Hare loped to the other end of the field while the Hedgehog took one step and stopped. When the Hare arrived at the end of the field, up popped Mrs Hedgehog.

"I am already here!" she said.

"Hey! What is this?" cried the Hare. "I was just warming up; let us race once more."

The Hare turned and ran, but much faster this time. When he arrived at the other end, the Hedgehog yelled, "I have been waiting for you for a long time."

"Just look at that," said the bewildered Hare. "Well, let us run again."

They both ran, and the Hare ran as fast as he could and, there at the end, was the Hedgehog again, but, of course, it was Mrs Hedgehog. The Hare ran back again and there was the Hedgehog waiting for him.

"I am already here!"

The Hare raced again and again, as fast as he was able. He ran some ninety-nine times and, after the hundredth time, he fell down in the field. After so much running, the poor fellow was so tired he could not even stand up.

"Never make fun of someone you think is weaker than you," said the Hedgehog, and he went home with his dear wife.

The Holy Icon

Times were hard, and the people were hungry. The rich landlords had plenty, as usual, but the peasants had nothing. There had not been much rain and the crops were poor. The people had almost given up hope.

In a certain village, there was a tavern not far from the church. It was a small village and, of course, the priest was well-acquainted with the tavern-keeper. One morning, the two met.

"Good morning, Father. How is attendance at church?"

"Not good. The people are miserable, and I fear they are losing faith in God."

"I have found the same thing at my place. We must be able to do something to wake up these people."

The two went into the tavern and put their heads together. They discussed the situation, and finally came up with a plan.

Next morning, the priest rode off to the city and bought a religious icon, a beautiful portrait of the Virgin Mary. Late that night, he returned to the village and carefully floated the picture on the water in the well.

At daybreak, a woman was at the well fetching water when she saw the icon floating there. She fell to her knees and crossed herself, then ran around the village yelling that there had been a miracle.

In no time at all, there was a crowd gathered at the well. Someone went to fetch the priest. When he heard what had happened, he began issuing orders:

"Let no one near the well. Ring the bell and tell everyone of our miracle."

The priest ran to the well, where he fell on his knees and proclaimed that a genuine miracle had taken place. He directed that a small chapel be built around the well and that the church was henceforth in charge of the site.

Soon, rumors began to be spread from the tavern that the water of the well had healing properties. It was said that a saint had appeared in the village, and now people with illnesses could be healed there. It was not long before people from all over the district were coming to see the well and get some of its magical water.

The church experienced a rebirth, as now there was proof of the greatness of God. The priest presided over a large congregation, and there was

once more money to fix the church and pay the priest for his services.

The tavern also experienced a resurgence of business. There were many pilgrims and travellers in town, and they ate, lodged and drank at the tavern.

One day, the tavern-keeper was listening to the talk in his tavern.

"This is my first visit here," said one man.

"This is my second visit," said another. "I came many miles to be healed."

"I am not so sure," said a third. "I do not think this is helping anybody."

The tavern-keeper stroked his beard and thought to himself, "Oh yes! At least two people are being helped: the priest and me!"

Ivan Pobyvan

A horrible, hungry Dragon had settled himself into a village and was destroying the place. He munched up all the people one by one, until there was only one old man left. The Dragon said to the old man, "Sleep well tonight, Dido, for tomorrow we shall have a nice feast." Then the Dragon laughed a booming laugh and swaggered off to have a sleep.

Later that evening, a young boy came striding past the ruined village. Seeing the old man, he stopped and said: "Good health to you, Dido. You appear to have had some excitement around here. But I am weary with travelling; do you perhaps have some space where I could spend the night?"

"What, are you tired of living?" the old man asked the boy.

"How do you mean?" asked the boy.

"There is a horrible Dragon here," said the old man. "He has eaten every one of the villagers but me, and I am on his menu for tomorrow."

"No, no," said the boy. "He will not eat you." He was so perky and full of confidence that Dido cheered up. The two of them went to some of the empty houses and had themselves a good meal, then went to sleep.

The next morning, the Dragon arrived and saw the boy. "Good," he cried. "I will have dessert as well!"

The boy stood in front of the Dragon and said firmly, "Do not be too sure of that."

"Oh ho! What is this?" said the Dragon with his head cocked on one side, and he peered at the boy with his tiny little eye. "Are you stronger than I am?"

"There is no doubt about that," replied the bold young fellow.

"Well, then," said the Dragon, "let us see how strong you are. Can you do this?" The Dragon picked up a rock and crushed it into powder. He let the powder run through his fingers, dusted off his hands and stood back.

"Peanuts," replied the boy. "I can squeeze a rock so hard that the water all runs out." Pretending to pick up a rock, he took a piece of cheese and squashed it in his little hand as hard as ever he could. The whey from the squeezed cheese eased with a wheeze like a breeze between his fingers.

"Well now, that is pretty good!" cried the Dragon. "Come with me and be my companion."

"Very well," said the boy, "but I insist on being the leader."

As the two of them left the village, the old man fell on his knees and thanked God for saving him.

"What is your name?" asked the Dragon.

"I am known as Ivan Pobyvan, the Mighty One," replied the boy.

The Dragon was getting more and more uneasy. He said to himself, "I certainly hope this Ivan Pobyvan does not turn on me and beat me!"

At lunchtime, the Dragon said, "I will get things ready and you go get a steer to cook."

Ivan went to the herd of cattle kept by the Dragon and looked at them. He knew that he would not be able to lift even one leg, let alone a whole steer. He walked in among the steers and began tying their tails together.

The Dragon heard the cattle bawling and went to see what was going on with his new companion. When he saw what the boy was doing, he stopped in amazement. "What on earth can you possibly be doing?" he asked.

"It is a waste of time to take just one or two steers," said Ivan. "I am going to take all of them to the house."

"No, no," said the Dragon. "If we eat them all up now, we will have nothing for tomorrow." He grabbed one steer and went home with it. He was really beginning to be afraid of this Ivan Pobyvan he had linked himself up with.

When the Dragon had prepared the steer, he fashioned a large bucket from its hide and tossed it on the ground in front of Ivan. "Bring it full of water," he said.

Ivan barely dragged the hide to the well and tipped it in. There was no way he was going to be able to pull that thing out again. He found

himself a stick and began to scratch at the earth beside the well.

The Dragon came out to see where Ivan had got to and, when he saw the boy with the stick, he asked, "Now what are you doing?"

"It is too much trouble to carry the water so far. I am going to move the whole well closer to the house."

The Dragon said, "Oh please, leave the well where it is. I will take the water myself. You go and get a nice big dry oak tree for the fire." He pulled the full hide out of the well and started back to the house.

"Why should I be bothered with only one tree?" cried Ivan angrily. "I suppose you would not like it if I tied all the forest together and took it to your house!"

"Oh, please do not be angry with me," said the Dragon. "I will do it." He ripped one oak tree out by the roots and carried both it and the water to the house.

Finally, the meal was ready and the Dragon began to devour the steer. The boy, knowing that he could not put on a good show of eating half a steer, pretended that he was still angry and refused to eat.

When there was only a very little bit left, Ivan took a few mouthfuls, sneered and said, "That is not much food!"

"Let us go to visit my mother," said the Dragon. "Perhaps she will prepare some potato varennyky for us."

They went to where Mother Dragon lived and she soon had boiled up twenty pots of varennyky. The Dragon greedily shovelled them into his mouth, while Ivan ate a few from his pot and stuffed the rest into his shirt.

When the pots were empty, the Dragon said to Ivan, "Let us go and roll around on that big rock to scratch our backs." The Dragon spun himself around and around on the rock, and sparks flew in all directions.

"Peanuts!" cried the boy. "Do it like this, so that the juices flow out of the rock." Ivan spun himself around on his stomach, squeezing the varennyky in his shirt, and their juice flew all around him.

"I am getting tired of your silly little games," said Ivan. "Let us now have a contest which I will propose. Let us see which of us can whistle the loudest."

The Dragon immediately let out an ear-splitting blast that knocked Ivan head over heels and bent the trees in the forest over so that they kissed the ground.

Ivan shook himself off and, when he got back to the Dragon, he said, "You had better hold your eyes and ears shut so that I do not blind you and deafen you."

The Dragon covered his eyes and ears, and Ivan picked up a big rock and brought it down on the top of the head of the Dragon with a loud hollow 'Klonggg!'

"You win, you win!" cried the Dragon. "You are too mean for me. I do not want to be your partner any more. I will build you a little house and you can live by yourself."

The Dragon built the house and then went to ask his mother what he could do to be rid of this Ivan Pobyvan. "When he is asleep tonight, burn him up in his house," said his mother.

Ivan overheard this conversation and, that night, he hid in the forest. After the house had completely burned to the ground, he went into the ruins and lay down in the warm ashes.

Next morning, the Dragon went to see what was left of his former partner, and was astounded to see him whole. Ivan stood up and brushed the ashes from his clothes. "I must have had too many blankets last night," he said. "It was so warm I could hardly sleep."

The Dragon ran babbling to his mother, and the two of them took to their heels. They were never seen in that part of the country again.

Kyrylo the Tanner

A long time ago, the Prince of Kyiv was troubled by a mighty Dragon who lived nearby. Each year, the Dragon demanded a tribute of one young boy or girl and, one year, he demanded the daughter of the Prince himself. The Prince had to comply, since his citizens had given up their own sons or daughters every year.

Reluctantly, the Prince embraced his daughter in a tearful farewell and sent her to the Dragon. The daughter was very beautiful, and the Dragon fell deeply in love with her. He treated the girl well enough, but she still longed to be with her own family. She began to plan how she might escape from the Dragon.

"Oh, mighty Dragon," she said, "you must be the strongest in all the world. Tell me truthfully; is there anyone as strong as you?"

"There is one man," replied the Dragon. "He is a tanner named Kyrylo who lives in Kyiv near the Dnipro River. When he builds his fire in the morning, the smoke rises to the sky. When he carries his hides to soak in the river, he carries not one or two, but twelve at a time.

"When the hides are soaked and he is pulling them from the river, I sometimes hide in the river and hold onto them, to test his strength. He has no trouble at all pulling them out, even with me hanging on with all my weight. He simply pulls on them, and I have to let go or he would pull me out, too. He is the only one in the world that I fear."

Later, when the Dragon was occupied elsewhere, the Princess wrote a letter to her father, telling him what the Dragon had said.

"Batko," she wrote, "please ask Kyrylo to fight the Dragon and set me free. Offer him whatever you wish, but mind how you approach him; he may be proud and easily offended."

The Princess tied the letter to the leg of her pet pigeon and sent him out of the window. The pigeon flew straight home to the castle of the Prince. The small children of the Prince were playing in the yard when the pigeon landed among them. "Tato, Tato!" cried the children. "This pigeon belongs to our sister."

The Prince, when he saw the pigeon, feared that the Dragon had killed the Princess. He took the pigeon from the children and found the letter. He read it quickly, and then called his entire court to meet in the Great Hall.

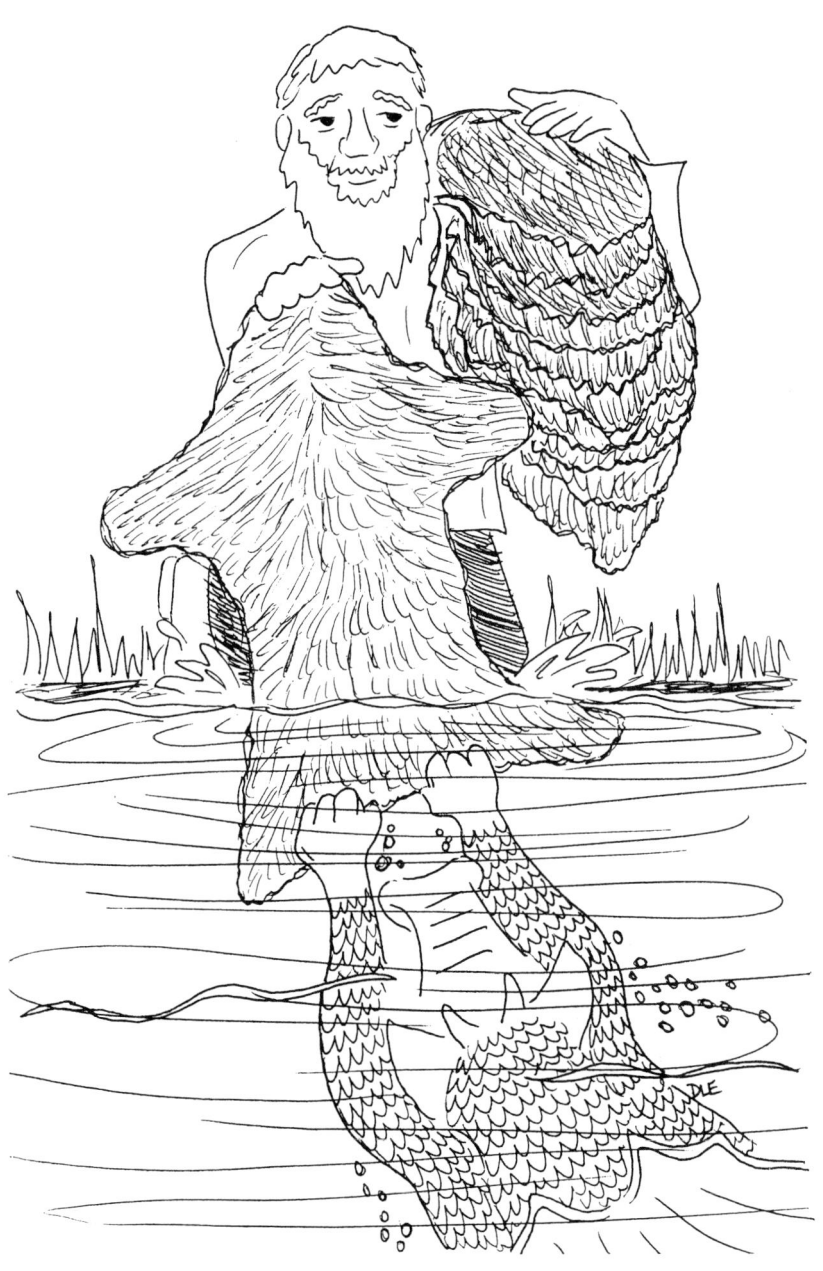

He read them her letter and asked, "Is there amongst us such a man as this Kyrylo?"

"There is, my Prince. He lives by the Dnipro River, and he is indeed a tanner."

"That is good. Now, how can we approach him to save our Princess?"

This was discussed for some time and, finally, it was decided that the two oldest people in the city would go to ask Kyrylo to fight the Dragon. The two oldest citizens were quickly found, and they agreed to take on the task.

The two had heard of Kyrylo and were frightened of him, but they went to his home and quietly pushed open the door. Kyrylo sat facing away from them; he was kneading twelve hides at once with his huge hands, and his whole body moved with the rhythm of his work.

The wind banged the door shut, and this so startled Kyrylo that he ripped all the hides at once. As he turned to look at them, the two bowed right down to the floor. "The Prince has sent us to you with a plea," they said.

Kyrylo was not listening; he just stared at them. They had made him ruin twelve hides. Finally, he told them to leave before he became angry. He had not heard one word they had said.

The two messengers hung their heads and went back to the castle to make their report. The Prince and his court then decided to send two young men to speak to Kyrylo.

The two young men went to Kyrylo, but he would not even allow them into his house. The despairing Prince then sent his own two young children to talk to Kyrylo.

The children kneeled in front of Kyrylo and tearfully told their story. Kyrylo listened quietly and, by the end of their tale, he was weeping along with them. "I will do this for you," he said.

Kyrylo went to the castle to make arrangements for the battle. "I will need twelve barrels of pitch and twelve wagonloads of hemp fibres," he told the Prince.

Kyrylo wound the hemp around his body, covered himself with pitch, and picked up his immense oaken club. He then went straight to the home of the Dragon, who said, "Well, Kyrylo. Have you come to fight or to visit?"

"I have not come to visit," said Kyrylo. "I have come to fight you."

A battle soon began which made the earth quake. The Dragon bit Kyrylo with his horrible teeth, but he chewed only chunks of hemp and pitch and, when Kyrylo hit him with his club, the blow was so mighty that he drove the Dragon into the ground.

The fight raged on and, finally, the two combatants paused to rest. The Dragon rushed to the river to drink some water to cool his overheated body, while Kyrylo wrapped more hemp and pitch about himself.

The battle soon resumed and, the more they fought and the more pitch the Dragon ate and the more Kyrylo clubbed him, the hotter the Dragon became. The next time they paused to rest, the Dragon again ran to the river to drink, but he was so hot that the water turned to steam inside him and he exploded.

The whole city had turned out to watch the battle, and they cheered and clapped with all their might. "Our Princess is saved! Hooray for Kyrylo! Hooray for our Hide-Twister!"

To honor Kyrylo and to commemorate the mighty battle, the Prince ordered that the place where Kyrylo lived be called 'Kozhemyaka,' which means 'Hide-Twister' or 'Tanner.' It is known by that name to this very day.

The Magic Chest

There were two brothers who lived in the same village. One brother was wealthy and the other was a poor man. One day, the poor man said to his rich brother: "You have much grain harvested. Let me thresh it for you, so that I can earn enough flour to make a paska for the Easter blessing tomorrow. My wife and I have no money to buy flour, and I have nowhere else to turn for help."

The wealthy brother thought a moment, then led the poor fellow to the barn, where he gave him a flail and said, "Here you are. Go to work, and come see me at the end of the day."

The poor man worked hard all day. He worked and worked, and had a great deal of the grain threshed by evening. He sought out his brother and said: "I have worked all day for you, and I have threshed a large pile of grain. I would like to take my flour and go home, as there is not much time to make the paska before morning."

The wealthy brother sneered at this and said: "You think you have earned a great deal for that little bit of work you did. To earn my flour you have to work for two whole days. When you have done so, I will pay you."

The poor man was so angry and frustrated that he went home in tears. When he got home, he told his wife what had happened. She was also disappointed in his brother, but said instead: "Go to the woods, my husband, and find us a piece of poplar wood. We can make a paska from the wood, and we can have that blessed. As long as it looks like a paska, it will be all right."

The man went to the woods and cut a piece of wood, which he carved into a smooth, round paska. His wife was delighted; she smeared it with egg to make it yellow and shiny. When it was finished, the paska was the most beautiful one they had ever seen.

Next morning, they took their paska to church. They placed it in a row with the others and stood waiting for it to be blessed. The rich brother would not lower himself to visit with the lesser people, so he sent his son to see what his poor brother had brought to be blessed.

The boy walked around the church, looking at everything. He spotted his uncle and the paska and ran back to his father. "Father! What a paska Vuiko has! I have never seen one that beautiful before. It is smooth and shiny and perfect in every way."

After the ceremony, the rich man could endure it no longer. He found his poor brother and said: "Brother, that is a fine paska. Sell it to me and I will invite you to my place for the feast. How much shall I pay you for it?"

Before the poor man could reply, he said, "Never mind, I will give you five gold coins for it." He tossed him five gold coins, took the paska, and rode home in his carriage, leaving his brother to make his way on foot.

By the time the poor fellow got to the home of his brother, the feast was over. There was nothing left to eat, and the poor brother went home hungry. He and his wife soon spent the five gold coins on food and clothing, and were once more destitute.

A few days later, the man was at the river looking for something to eat when he spied a crab sitting in the sun. He was hungrily staring at the crab when it spoke to him: "Why are you so sad, my good man?"

The man was amazed to hear the crab speak but, after he regained his wits, he sat down and told the crab his whole story.

When the crab had heard him out, he said, "Cheer up, for I can give you something that will make you happy." He slipped into the river and soon came back with a small chest grasped in his claws. "Here you are, my friend. Take this magic

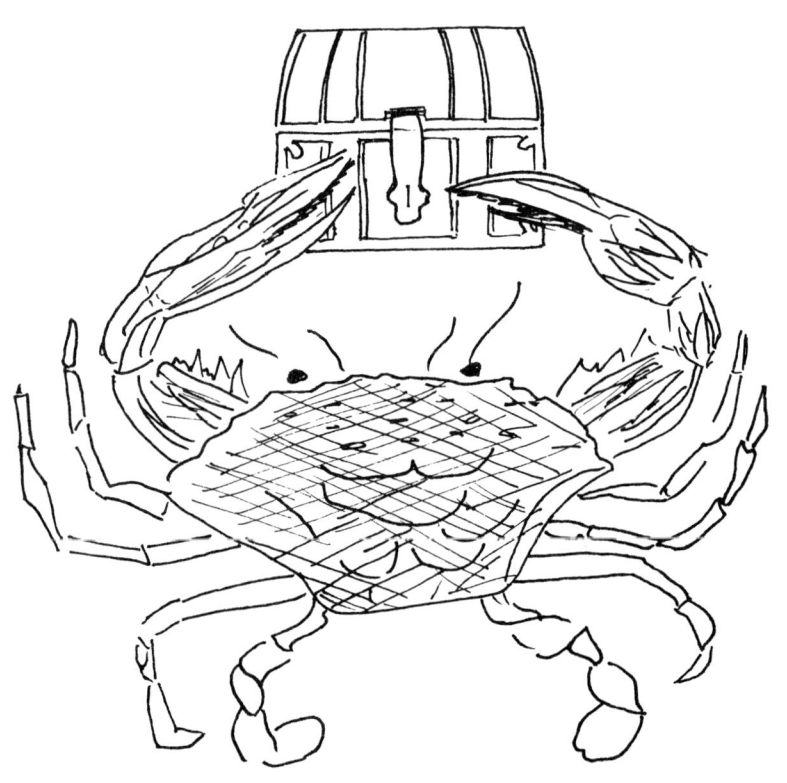

chest home and say, 'Little chest, open!' It will open, and it will be full of everything you may wish for. When you have taken out what you need, say, 'Little chest, close!' and it will close up and wait for you."

The man thanked the crab, picked up the chest and went home. When he got home, his wife and children gathered about asking, "What is it? What do you have, Tato? What is in it?"

"I myself do not know what I have here. Little chest, open!"

As soon as he said that, the chest popped open. It was full of many fine things. There was food, and there was clothing enough for everyone. The happy family rejoiced in their good fortune. They ate heartily and then dressed in their new clothes.

The children of the wealthy brother rode by later and saw their cousins well-dressed and playing happily. "Where did you get the fine clothes?" they asked.

"Tato brought home a wonderful chest!" they exclaimed. "When it opened, we found fine clothes and much wonderful food inside. We ate our fill and dressed ourselves, and the chest still holds much more!"

The wealthy cousins raced home and told their father what they had seen and heard. He leapt up and immediately rode out to see for himself. How could it be that his poor brother had such a thing and he had not?

"Glory to God!" he greeted his poor brother.

"Glory forever!" was the reply.

"What is new with you, my brother?"

"We are happy enough," replied the poor man. "Now we can live a little."

"My children said that you have some kind of a little chest full of things."

"Yes, that is true."

"Where did you get something like that?"

"God gave it to us."

"I think I would like to have that chest," said the rich man. "I will pay you five hundred gold coins for it."

The poor man was dazzled by the offer. He had never even dreamed of so much gold and, not knowing what he was doing, he sold the chest to his brother. The rich man took the chest and went home, where he told it to open and close as his brother had showed him, and was well pleased with his purchase.

The poor man, suddenly rich beyond his dreams, did not have any idea how to handle his wealth, and he let it all slip away, bit by bit.

Later, when he finally realized what he had done, the poor man was again by the river. The crab called to him and said, "Hello! Are you still sad, even with such a fine little chest?"

The poor fellow told the crab what had happened. "I was overwhelmed by dreams of gold and, like a fool, I sold the chest to my sly brother. Now here I am, poor again and hungry."

"That is bad news," said the crab. "But I can help you once more. I will give you another chest, but a different one. This is the last one I have, though, so do the right thing with it."

"What does one do with this little chest?" asked the man.

"To open it you say, 'Out of the drum, boys!' To close it up, you whistle."

The happy man ran home, called his family together, and put the chest on the table. He stood back and said, "Out of the drum, boys!" Instantly, the lid flew open and out streamed a band of Cossacks with whips and clubs. They beat the poor man, they beat the poor woman, and they beat the poor children. They chased them all over the house, whipping and beating them.

The stunned man finally remembered to whistle, and all the Cossacks jumped back into the chest. When everyone had calmed down somewhat and the man had regained his wits, he thought to himself, "I must sell this chest to my wicked brother. He is much tempted by such things, and it will teach him a lesson."

The rich man, with the help of his children, had been keeping an eye on his brother. When the children came running home with the news that they had seen their uncle with another chest, he immediately rode out to visit. "How are things with you, brother?" he asked.

"Things are fine, brother," was the reply.

"I hear you have another little chest."

"Yes, that is true."

"I would like to buy this chest from you."

"Well, why not?" said the poor brother. "I still have need of money. This chest is not like the other one, though. This one will cost one thousand gold coins."

The rich brother was drunk with greed. What riches could be here in this chest? He counted out the coins with shaking hands and, as he was counting, asked his brother how to open the chest. His avarice had such a hold on him that he never thought to ask about closing it.

The poor man said, "To open the chest you say, 'Out of the drum, boys!' and it will open."

The rich man sped away with his new possession. When he got home, he ran into the house, put the chest on the table, assembled his entire household and commanded, "Out of the drum, boys!" In an instant, the band of Cossacks streamed out of the chest with whips and clubs, and they began to beat everyone in sight.

The rich man hid under the table, his wife cowered in the corner, the children and servants ran screaming around the room, and the band of Cossacks continued to beat and lash them all.

"Stop!" pleaded the rich man. "Into the drum, boys! Close, little chest! Help!" Nothing worked, and he feared for his very life.

Finally, one of the children fell through a window. Finding himself outside, he ran for all he was worth to his uncle. "Vuiko! Come quick!

Cossacks came out of the little chest, and they are beating everybody without mercy!"

"Is that so?" said the poor man. "Well, I suppose I must come. But let me find my boots. And where did I put my hat?"

"Hurry, Vuiko, hurry, or we will not find anybody left alive!"

They finally arrived at the home of the rich man, and what a commotion! They could hear yelling and thumping and screaming and cries of "Into the drum, boys!"

The poor man walked into the house and whistled. Suddenly all was still, except for the moaning and the groaning. Everyone in the house was severely beaten. They were lying everywhere, battered and bleeding and barely breathing. The poor man told the child to run for the doctor, then he went home.

A couple of days later, the rich man asked his brother to come to him. The poor man went to see his brother, who was in bed in bad shape.

"That was a very nasty trick you played on me," he said to the poor man.

"No," said his brother. "That, you earned yourself. You cheated me when I threshed your grain, you invited me to your feast knowing full well that I could not get there until it was over, and then you tricked me with your gold when you bought my other chest.

"Also, when I got this chest to replace the other one, I took a beating from the Cossacks until

I learned what the chest was really for. I place that beating on your account, too.

"Now I will take these two chests home. If you ever again come to do me harm, I will release the Cossacks, and you will be sorry."

The poor man picked up the two chests and went home. The rich man lay in bed for a few days, then a few weeks, then a few months, and he never again rose from his bed to do evil to his brother, or to anyone else.

Okh

This story happened a long, long time ago, beyond our memory, before our fathers and even before our grandfathers had been born. At this time, there lived a poor couple and their son Ivan, who was nothing like a normal son. He was so lazy that he never did any work. He would not go for water or cut wood or do anything. He just sat on the pich and played with millet seeds, sifting them from one hand to the other.

The boy was twenty years old, but he had spent almost all of those years sitting on the warm pich. If someone gave him something to eat, he ate; if not, he went without.

The parents were worried about their son. "What shall we do with you?" they asked. "You do not want to work; you are completely useless. Other children help their parents, but you just sit on the warm pich and eat bread."

The parents worried for a long time and, at last, the mother asked the father, "What do you think we should do with our son Ivan?"

"Perhaps we should send him away from home. It may be that a stranger could teach him how to work."

Next day, the father took the boy to a tailor, to see if he could learn that trade. Ivan stayed for three days and ran back home.

Father gave his son a beating and next day sent him to a shoemaker. The lad stayed with the shoemaker a couple of days and ran back home again, where he got another beating. He was then sent to a blacksmith but, again, ran away home to another beating.

Finally, the father said, "I will take our useless son far, far away to another country. There, even if he cannot be hired out, at least he cannot run home."

The father took Ivan and led him away until they entered a forest so thick that they could see only the earth below and a bit of sky above. They were tired and, when they reached a burned-out stump by the side of the path, the father said, "I must rest. I will sit on this stump for a while. Okh! I am exhausted."

Just as he said these words, a dwarf came out of the stump. His face was wrinkled and a green beard hung down to his knees. "What do you want of me?" he asked.

"What is this?" cried the man in surprise. "What do you want? Keep away from me!"

"Why, you called me," said the dwarf. "Now, what do you want?"

"I called you? No, I did no such thing!" protested the poor confused man.

"You say you did not call me, but I know that you did."

"Who are you?" asked the man.

"I am Okh, the Forest King," said the dwarf. "Now, why did you call me?"

"I did not even think of calling you," replied the man.

"Yes, you did call me. I heard you, plain as plain. You called, 'Okh!'"

"Oh, that!" said the man. "I was tired, and that is what one says when one is tired. I certainly did not mean to call you."

"Well, here I am, anyway. Who are you and where are you going?" asked Okh.

"Just anywhere," said the man. "I am taking my son to be hired out. I am hoping that strangers can teach him to work because, at home, he does nothing and, when I hire him out, he runs away."

"Hire him out to me," said the dwarf. "I will teach him some of the many useful things that I can do. There is one condition, though; he will have to stay with me for one whole year. When you come for him, if you recognize him after that one year, he can go home with you. If not, he will have to stay with me another year."

"Good," said the man. The deal was made and the father went home.

Okh led young Ivan to his home, which was in the other world beneath the earth. They came to a little green hut covered with reeds. Everything in the hut was green. The walls were green, the floor and ceiling were green, the furniture was green, even his wife and children were green. His maids were water nymphs and they, too, were green as rue.

"Sit down, my hired man, and have something to eat," said Okh.

The water nymphs brought some food, which was also green. After they had eaten, Okh said, "Go and cut some firewood and bring it here into my hut."

Ivan went to the woodpile, looked at it for a moment, and lay down beside it to sleep. Okh came to see how the boy was working, and found him asleep. He woke him up and ordered him to stack the wood right there. When the wood was stacked, Okh placed the boy on the top of the pile and set fire to it.

When the wood and Ivan had burned completely, Okh scattered the ashes in the wind. One glowing ember fell to the ground, and Okh sprinkled some Water of Life on it. In a twinkling, the young lad was standing there alive and healthy.

The only difference was that now he appeared to be a bit more lively.

Okh ordered the boy to cut more firewood, and went back to his hut. Ivan lay down and went to sleep again. Okh found him sleeping and burned him again. He scattered the ashes in the wind and revived one glowing ember. Again, the young fellow stood there alive and healthy.

Ivan had improved considerably, but he still went to sleep when Okh left him to cut the wood. A third time, he was burned up and revived. This time, he became a fine figure of a young man and very alert.

Although this process took only one day in the world of the dwarf, one entire year had passed in the world above, and the father came to claim his son. He sat on the stump and called out, "Okh! Okh!"

The dwarf appeared and said, "Good day and good health to you."

"Good health to you too, Okh."

"What do you want?" asked Okh.

"I have come for my son."

"Come with me. If you recognize your son, you may have him. If not, he must stay with me one more year."

The man went with Okh to his little green hut. There, Okh opened a bag of millet seed and strewed it all over the floor. Immediately, a flock of roosters gathered and began pecking at the seed. "Do you recognize your son?" asked Okh.

The father stared and stared at the roosters, but they were all alike and he could not guess which one it could be. Okh said, "Go back home, as you did not recognize your son. Return in one year."

When the father returned the next year, Okh led him to a sheepfold full of identical rams. Once again, the father could not pick out his son and had to go home without him.

After the third year, the father was walking towards the stump when he met an old man who was as white as milk, including his hair, his skin and his clothes. "Good health to you, Dido," he said to the white man.

"Good health to you, too," said the old man. "Where are you off to today?"

"I am going to Okh to try to claim my son from bondage."

"What is this bondage all about?" asked the old white man.

When he had heard the whole story, the old man said, "This is not good. I know Okh and, although he is not really evil, he will be leading you by your nose for a long, long time."

"I am beginning to see that," said the father, "but what can I do? How can I recognize my son when Okh plays such tricks?"

"I know how," said the old man.

"Please tell me, Dido. In spite of what the boy was like, he is still my son, and I would like to free him."

"Listen well to what I say: when you come to Okh, he will release many pigeons; the pigeon who is your son will be sitting under the pear tree, preening himself."

Thanking the old white man, the father went to the stump and called, "Okh! Okh!"

Okh appeared and led the father into his kingdom. He scattered some grain on the ground and called his pigeons. A hundred identical pigeons flew down to peck at the wheat. "Which is your son? If you can tell me, you may have him. If not, he is mine for another year."

All the pigeons were feeding on the wheat, except for one who was sitting under the pear tree, preening himself. The father said, "That one under the pear tree is my son."

"I do not know how you could tell, but you have guessed correctly," said Okh. "You may take your son home." He waved his hand, and the pigeon turned into a fine-looking youth.

The father and son were very happy to see each other, and embraced tearfully. "Let us go home," said the father, and they departed.

While walking along, they discussed what had happened. The father asked, "How was it working for that Okh?"

Ivan told his father all that had happened to him, and the father then said, "Ivan, I am poor and you also are poor. You have just worked for three years and have earned nothing. I do not know what the future holds for all of us."

"Do not worry, father," said Ivan. "I have learned some things from Okh. Look there across the field; the sons of the boyar are getting ready for a fox hunt. I will turn myself into a greyhound and catch the fox. Then everybody will want to buy me from you. Sell me to them for three hundred gold pieces, but be sure that I am sold without the leash."

Suddenly, there was a great clamor, and the hunt was on. Ivan changed himself into a greyhound, joined the hunt and, eventually, caught the fox. The young noblemen had never seen that greyhound before, and they asked the father if it was his. "Yes, it is mine," he said.

"That is a fine hound," they said. "Will you sell him to us?"

"Yes, for three hundred gold pieces, but he is to be sold with no leash."

"We do not need your leash; we will get him a golden one. We will give you one hundred gold pieces for him."

"No," said the father. "My price is three hundred; no more, no less."

"Very well, here is your money." They took the hound and went after another fox. The new hound chased the fox into the forest, changed back to a man, and returned to his father.

The father and son walked towards home, and the father said, "What shall we do with this money? There is enough to repair our house, but there will not be much left over."

"Fear not, father," said Ivan. "There will be plenty more. There in the field, the boyars are hunting quail with falcons. I will become a falcon, and they will want to buy me. Tell them you will sell me for three hundred gold pieces, but without the hood which they put over the head of the bird when he is not hunting."

As they watched, a boyar released a falcon. The falcon chased a quail all over the sky, but was unable to catch it. Ivan changed himself into a falcon and instantly was upon the quail.

"Is this your falcon that has done this?" asked the boyar of the father.

"Yes, it is," replied the father.

"Sell him to us."

"Very well. My price is three hundred gold pieces, without the hood."

"What do we need with such a cheap hood? We will get him a hood of brocade," said the hunters, and the deal was made. They sent the falcon after a quail. He chased the quail into the forest, where he reverted to his human form.

He rejoined his father, who said, "You were right, Ivan. Now we are in much better shape."

"There will be more, father. We are coming to the market; I will change into a horse, and you will sell me. Ask for one thousand gold pieces, but sell me without the bridle."

Before they got to the market, Ivan changed himself into a wild, high-spirited stallion. The father led the prancing, pawing horse into the market, and the people scattered in front of such a fiery steed. In no time at all, there was a large circle of excited people around the horse, and the trading began.

"I want one thousand gold pieces for this horse, without the bridle," announced the father.

"That is too much," said one horse-trader. "Besides, what do we need with your bridle? They are easy to get. I will give you five hundred for the horse."

"No," said the father. "My price is firm. I ask one thousand gold pieces; I ask no more and I ask no less."

A one-eyed gypsy came to the front of the crowd. "I will give you five hundred for the horse and the bridle," he said.

"No deal," said the father. "My price is one thousand, without the bridle."

"Well then," said the gypsy. "I will give you six hundred gold pieces. That is a good deal of money; take it."

They bargained back and forth for some time and, finally, the gypsy said, "Very well, I will give you one thousand but, for that price, I will have the bridle, too."

"No, I am afraid not," said the father. "The bridle is mine."

"My good man," said the gypsy, "where did you ever see a horse sold without the bridle? Certainly it is not worth it to you to lose such a good deal for an old bridle."

"Say what you will," answered the father. "The bridle is mine."

The gypsy would not let the matter drop. He argued and begged and threatened and, finally, offered the father five gold pieces for the bridle. The father was not used to such pressure, and he finally agreed, saying to himself, "I am not enjoying this at all, at all. And the gypsy is right. This old bridle is certainly not worth more than three gold pieces."

"We have a deal," he said to the gypsy. He took the money, turned over the horse and bridle, and went home.

The gypsy rode off on the horse and, when they were deep in the forest, he jumped onto the ground and turned himself back into Okh the Forest King, for that is who he really was. He laughed mightily, for he had played a real trick on young Ivan and his father!

Okh the dwarf rode Ivan the horse a long, long way. They rode higher than the trees and lower than the clouds; they rode along the river and through the valley. Finally, they arrived at the green home of the Forest King.

Okh stabled the horse and went into his hut. "He did not get away from me, after all, that son of a dog," he chortled.

After lunch, Okh led the horse to the river to water him. They had just reached the river when Ivan the horse turned into a perch and leaped into the water. Okh changed himself into a pike and swam after the perch. He could swim faster than the perch, but he was not as agile. He would just about grab the perch when Ivan would stretch his fins and turn on his tail. The pike could not catch the perch.

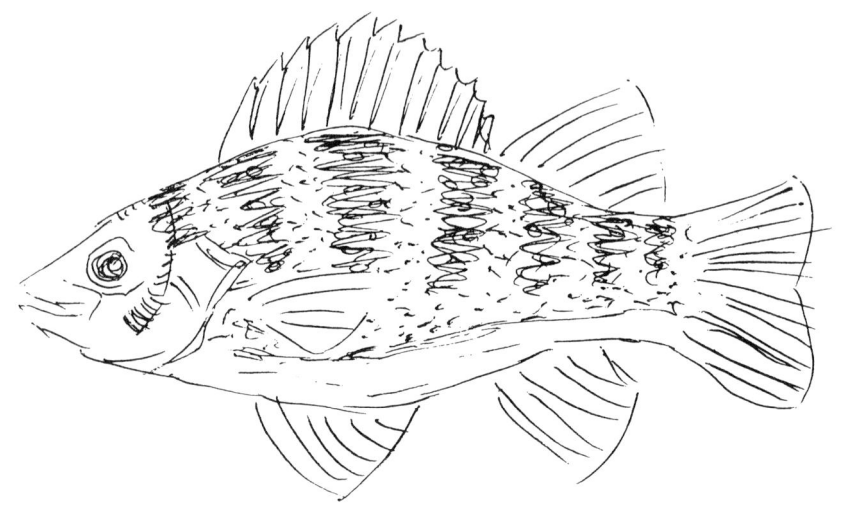

"Stop," said Okh the pike. "I would like to talk to you."

"I can hear you well enough without stopping," said Ivan the perch.

Okh chased and chased Ivan, but simply could not catch him. At last, the perch swam to the riverbank, where a tsarevna was rinsing her kerchief in the water. He jumped out of the water and, while he was in the air, turned into a garnet ring set in gold.

The tsarevna spotted the ring in the water, picked it up, and fitted it onto her finger. Later, at home, she said to her father, "Look, Batko, what a beautiful ring I have found!"

A footman came and said that there was a trader in the yard who wished to speak with the tsar. Of course, the trader was Okh in disguise again. The tsar asked, "What is it you want?"

"I was sailing up the river when I lost a garnet ring set in gold, and I want to know if any of your people have found it," he said.

"Yes," said the tsar. "My daughter, the tsarevna, found such a ring."

Okh demanded that the tsarevna return the ring. He said, "You have something which is rightfully mine, and you must return it to me."

The tsarevna did not much care for the trader, and she refused to give it to him. Her father said, "Give him the ring, Dochechka. We must do what is right."

"I will give you anything I own," said the trader, "but you cannot have the ring."

"If that is so," said the tsarevna, "then you shall not have it, either." She took off the ring and threw it on the floor, and it shattered. The many pieces of the ring scattered like millet seeds all over the floor.

Okh immediately changed himself into a rooster and began pecking at the millet. He picked up all the seeds, except for one which had rolled under the right shoe of the tsarevna. When he was satisfied that he had all the seeds, Okh flew out of the window.

The one hidden millet seed turned into a young man, so handsome that the tsarevna fell in love with him instantly. "I must marry this man," she said. "He is my good fortune, and I can never be happy with anyone else."

The tsar frowned. This man was obviously a peasant; how could he give his daughter to such a poor man? The tsarevna insisted; her mother, the tsarina, added her blessings and, eventually, the tsar relented. "Well, maybe we can make something of this young man," he said.

Ivan brought his mother and father to the palace to live, and he and the tsarevna were soon married. The wedding was so grand that everybody was invited, except for Okh.

A Visit in the Grave

A long time ago in Ukraine, peasants had to work for a wealthy master or landlord in order to survive. In those days, the lord of a village actually owned the people who worked for him, in much the same way that he owned his cattle. Often, too, the lord would treat his people in the same manner as he treated his cattle.

Ostap and Ivan were two such peasants, unfortunate enough to be born into a family who owned nothing. As a result, they were bonded for life to a rich and cruel landlord, who would beat his people with no thought for them at all.

Ostap and Ivan were close brothers. Their family had all died in the service of the lord, which drew the two even closer together. They could not have been closer had they been twins. What little they possessed belonged to both equally, and there never passed between them an unkind word.

The two had little joy in their lives. Their happiest moments were those when they paused to rest while working, and their eyes met. Then they would smile with the love in their hearts that comes from being so close.

Life was hard, hard. The brothers worked every day of their lives, with no days free to themselves. If the landlord was unhappy for any reason, it was not unusual for him to beat whoever happened to be nearby. Often enough, it was one brother or the other who was beaten.

Ostap was the elder brother and, being smaller and not as strong as Ivan, he suffered greatly from these beatings. Finally, the lord beat him too much, and Ostap collapsed and died right there in the field.

Ivan sadly buried his brother and continued to work, as there was nothing else he could do. He was miserably unhappy. Often, in his dreams, he would turn and look back down the furrow and see Ostap standing there with the plow in his hand, smiling at him. He was so lonesome and unhappy that he thought he might as well die, just as his brother had done.

One day, Ivan was sitting with his meagre lunch, watching the other workers who sat eating with their wives or husbands. The thought struck him that, even if times are so bad, it would be easier for two to bear up than one. He would marry, and then he would no longer be so alone.

He made it known that he wanted to marry, and this was soon arranged.

Ivan went to the grave of his brother, as he often did, for he still missed him dearly. He kneeled on the grave and wept as he planted an acorn as a remembrance.

"Ostap, my dear brother, please honor me with your presence at my wedding," he said through his tears.

No sooner had he uttered these words than the grave opened wide, and Ostap stood there, smiling as he used to.

"Good health to you, brother," said Ostap. "Come in and visit."

Ivan stepped into the grave, which closed behind him like a door. He and his beloved brother were standing in a little room with a candle burning brightly.

"How are things in your life?" asked Ostap.

"Things are as they ever were," replied Ivan. "Life is hard, and I miss you terribly. I must work for two of us now that you are no longer with me, and I do not know how much more I can take."

"Yes, our life on earth is a sad affair. But here, listen and I will read to you how life can be if we live according to the ways of God."

Taking up a large book, Ostap began to read. He read the words in the book, which told of how life could be and should be.

"Love there must be," he read. "Love and kindness above all. There must be peace among people, and no one person should be thought better than any other person. There must be laughter in the world, and everybody must live as we once did, as brothers."

The candle burned low as Ostap read, and he lit another one. He read on and on and, as he lit yet a third candle, Ivan said,

"Read more, dear Ostap. I would like to live in such a world." His eyes streamed tears as he thought of how hard life on earth was and how good it could be.

Ostap read on of the world as it ought to be. There was no war, there was no quarrelling, and people shared freely with their neighbors. There was no sadness, and all lived like children, trusting each other and God. Finally, the third candle burned out.

"I must go," Ivan said, "although I could listen to you read for three hundred years. But I must go now to be married."

The brothers stood up and embraced as the grave opened. Ivan turned and stepped out, and was once more in the world above.

As Ivan knelt to say farewell to his brother, he saw beside him the rotted-out stump of a huge oak tree.

"I do not remember this stump," thought Ivan. He stood and looked about him. "And I do not remember so many graves in this cemetery."

Walking back to the village, Ivan thought that things looked somehow different. He knew the road well enough, but it was not quite the same. Some of the huts in the village were familiar to him, but many more were not. He did not recognize anybody, not even the old people he met on his way. And they all looked at him strangely, as though he did not belong there.

Ivan finally came to the place where he thought his hut should be. There, he found an empty lot and some workmen preparing the spot for a building.

"What have you done with my house?" cried Ivan.

"What house?" asked one of the men. "This space has been empty for many years, and now the lord said we are to build him a granary."

"But where is my house?" asked Ivan. "It was here yesterday when I went to invite my brother to my wedding, and now it is not here!"

"What are you saying?" replied the man. "There once may have been a hut on this spot, but that was long ago. There has been no house here while I have been alive, and I was born in this village. But who are you? From where do you come, and what do you want in our village?"

"My name is Ivan, and yesterday I lived in this village. I went to the grave of my poor dead brother Ostap, and invited him to my wedding. I then must have fallen asleep, and today I recognize no one in my village."

"I have heard that story," said one of the workmen who had gathered around. "It is an old story. One brother named Ivan went to visit the grave of his brother Ostap, and that was the last anyone saw of either. The old people say this happened three hundred years ago."

"Whoever you are, old-timer, you must have heard the story somewhere, and now you are trying to make fools of us," said another man.

Ivan tried to say that his story was true, but the workmen just laughed and jeered at him. Some children appeared and they, too, began to make fun of Ivan.

Bewildered, Ivan kept insisting that what he said was true. With the band of mocking children following him, he wandered through the village looking for someone who would listen to his story. But he found no one he knew, and no one was interested in him.

Slowly, Ivan began to realize what had happened. While he was in the grave listening to Ostap read, time in the world above had not stood still, and each burning candle had marked the passage of one hundred years.

Remembering what Ostap had read from his book, Ivan tried to tell the people of the village of the wonderful way the world could be. People could live peacefully and without sorrow, hunger or fear.

Ivan found no one who would listen to him. Everyone was busy with their own affairs, and no one had time to listen to this strange old man with the strange old story.

Ivan travelled from village to village, trying to explain to people that life could be good, but nobody was interested. One day, he found himself back near his old home. Here, late on a cold evening, in his own village, there was no welcome for him. He stood in the road and thought and thought.

Finally, he returned to the cemetery, where he kneeled on the grave of his brother and said tearfully, "Ostap, I beg of you, let me in. I am so tired, and this world no longer has a place for me."

The grave opened, and Ostap welcomed his brother Ivan with open arms and a big smile.

"Welcome, my dear brother," he said. "Come in and we will read from the book."

Now, while the earth above goes on as badly as ever it has, Ostap and Ivan sit at the table and read to each other. As each candle flickers and dies, another one hundred years has passed, and the world has become that much older — but no wiser.

Zhabka

One day long ago, Zhabka, the little frog, was hopping about in the wide world looking for adventure. Coming upon a wooden bucket filled with fresh cream, he jumped in to see what kind of thing this was. He smiled to himself, because the funny white water felt so cool and silky against his skin.

He swam and splashed and dove until he had had enough. He was tired of the white water, and he wanted to go home and go to sleep. But then, Zhabka found he could not get out of the bucket. The cream was too deep for his legs to reach the bottom and jump, and the sides of the bucket were too slippery to climb out.

Zhabka was thunderstruck. It was hard to believe that a moment ago he was having such a good time! He could not bear the thought of drowning, so he kept swimming, hoping that he would think of something.

The little frog swam to his left; he swam to his right; and he swam around and around until he was too tired to move. He began to sink but, as he dropped beneath the surface, he spluttered, "No, I will not quit!" And he began to swim once more.

When he became too tired to move, Zhabka stopped to rest again and, once more, he sank beneath the surface. But, once more, he rose up and carried on swimming.

This happened several times until, one time when he sank, he felt something beneath his legs. He pushed down and hopped straight out of the bucket.

Without knowing what he had done, Zhabka had churned the cream so long that he had made a large, firm, yellow ball of butter beneath his legs!

Notes on the Tales

In the first volume of this series, *The Raspberry Hut*, several stories were translated from a battered old book my grandfather had given to my father. The covers and the first few pages of the book are missing, which makes it difficult to identify properly. However, it seems now that this old book is called *Fables and Stories Volume 2*, and it was printed in Winnipeg in the early 1900s. Interestingly enough, *Fables and Stories Volume 1* has recently come to light, and it also has the covers and the first few pages missing. Those stories will be translated and will appear in future volumes of this series.

In the acknowledgments at the beginning of this book, thanks are given to Professor Rudnyckyj and Dr Klymasz for material they had published and allowed me to use. Both of these people spent many long hours in the field, collecting stories from those who still were able to tell them. They both published some of their work in English, which made it perfect for my research. Thank you both for leading the way.

Some of their stories are unique in that I have found them only in the collections of these two authors. Nobody else seems to know the stories, or if they had known them, they had not written them down. If these stories had not been recorded by Professor Rudnyckyj and Dr Klymasz, they could have been lost forever. To me, that would have been a tragedy.

Their books are:

-*Ukrainian-Canadian Folklore in English Translation* by JB Rudnyckyj, published in Winnipeg in 1960 by UFAS.

-*Folk Narrative Among Ukrainian-Canadians in Western Canada* by Robert B Klymasz, published in Ottawa in 1973 by The National Museum of Man.

Many other books written by many other authors contain folk tales similar to some of those found in my collection. A complete list of the sources of my stories, along with a list of books containing similar stories, will be published when my collection is complete.

Notes on the Tales in This Volume

Page 11   The Adopted Father
This tale was translated by my father, from a collection of Ukrainian folk tales. It is found in several Ukrainian-language collections. Similar versions are also found in several English-language books. Sometimes the story is called "Three Brothers."

Page 21   Adventure in the Woods
This story comes from Professor Rudnyckyj's collection. It seems to be a Canadian adaptation of the animal tales found in every culture, in which 'good' individuals are treated well by supposedly vicious animals. I have seen this particular tale only this once, although there are bound to be similar stories elsewhere. This story supposedly took place in the bush country of Manitoba, where many Ukrainians farmed.

Page 25   The Bear and the Fiddler
Through much of history, the majority of the people of Ukraine have been subjected to tyranny and oppression by not only invaders, but also by the so-called higher classes of their own society. As a result, there are many folk tales in which the little fellow outsmarts the big guy or the authority figure. This is one way of feeling better about one's own miserable situation; if one cannot actually do these things, there is nothing to prevent one from telling a story about them.

In this story, the authority figure is represented by the bear. The poor peasant outsmarts the bear and escapes from his fate by using nothing more than his own wits. Plus, there is a familiar moral: Do not try to be what you are not.

Page 29   The Big Round Bun
Found in numerous collections, with varying details, this little story is a very common one. In English folklore, it parallels the story of "The Gingerbread Boy" or "The Gingerbread Man."

Page 35   Danylo Burmylo, the Bear
In folk tales, there is nothing unusual about men and animals talking together. In this tale we learn something about the life of a bear and also are reminded of the moral: Do not try to be what you are not.

Page 40   The Dog and the Wolf
This is another fairly common story. Sometimes it is called "Sirko," which is the dog's name. The name possibly could come from the Ukrainian word meaning grey, the color of the dog's coat. It also could be that part of this story has a basis in fact. It is possible that there was once a real dog that saved its master's child from a wolf, and every time the story was told, it picked up a few more details until we arrive at the present telling of the tale.

Page 47   The Goat and the Ram
There are many stories about odd pairings of animals. In some stories, supposedly mortal enemies work happily together, while in others such as this one, the friends are similar to each other. These two, a goat and a ram, are merely

acting like most goats and rams do, until they are thrown out into the world, where they survive all the unusual events by relying on their own inborn strengths.

Page 53   The Greedy Daughters
From Dr Klymasz's collection. This story could be true; all of the events are believable. It is a simple story of a wronged individual forcing others to do what is right by playing on the wrong-doers' own weaknesses and shortcomings. "It serves them right!"

Page 56   The Hedgehog and the Hare
This is similar to Aesop's famous tale of "The Tortoise and the Hare," where the slow but steady tortoise beats the smart-alecky hare in a race. This tale adds another dimension in its admonition to be polite to others.

Page 61   The Holy Icon
There are many tales with themes relating to religion in one form or another. Sometimes the stories are critical of the clergy and of the church in general. Often, however, the village priest was just as poorly-off as most of his parishioners, and had to make his living by using his wits. In this story, hard times are overcome with the help of a fake miracle. Such things have been known to happen. So far, I have found this story only in Dr Klymasz's book.

Page 65   Ivan Pobyvan
A young boy getting the better of a slow-witted dragon is not unusual in folklore. This particular boy is as full of spunk and as brazen as they come. There are many elements found in similar stories, and the whole tale glows with good humor and fun.

Page 75   Kyrylo the Tanner
Reluctant heroes are not uncommon. They can be persuaded to do the right thing, if only one knows how to approach them. Kyrylo is such a one. He is strong and to be feared, but he will help those who ask him properly. The dragon is the usual bad character found in many tales.

Page 83   The Magic Chest
This is another fairly common tale found in several books, including Dr Klymasz's collection. In some books, the story is identified as Russian. In the story, the little fellow bests the authority figure, who gets what he deserves, through a combination of the little fellow's good luck and his ability to make use of his luck.

Page 94   Okh
A fairly popular Ukrainian story. In English translations, the dwarf is often named 'Oh,' probably to make it easier to pronounce his name. We find all kinds of magic in this tale, and like usually happens, the good guy wins.

Page 113   A Visit in the Grave
This is my personal favorite. It says much about Ukrainian history and about the world in general. Times were very hard for the poorer people, but they always had hope that the future would be better. This seems to be a relatively little-told tale, but it is powerful and moving, though it is not a very happy story.

Page 125   Zhabka
A cute little story that teaches us a lesson. Never give up, even when things look their blackest. By persevering, the little frog saves himself, even though he may never know how he did it.

— Danny Evanishen, Editor

In this glossary:

[a] is pronounced as in f<u>a</u>r
[e] is pronounced as in g<u>e</u>t
[ee] is pronounced as in f<u>ee</u>t
[i] is pronounced as in s<u>i</u>t
[o] is pronounced as between g<u>o</u>t and g<u>oa</u>t
[oo] is pronounced as in l<u>oo</u>se
[y] is pronounced as in <u>y</u>es

[kh] is pronounced as in Scottish lo<u>ch</u>
[zh] is pronounced as in vi<u>s</u>ion